T0085664

eries

Mein erster Mozart
My First Mozart

Die leichtesten Klavierwerke von
Easiest Piano Works by
Wolfgang Amadeus Mozart

Herausgegeben von / Edited by
Wilhelm Ohmen

Coverillustration: Katharina Drees

ED 22062
ISMN 979-0-001-20115-5

www.schott-music.com

Mainz · London · Madrid · Paris · New York · Tokyo · Beijing
© 2015 Schott Music GmbH & Co. KG, Mainz · Printed in Germany

Wolfgang Amadeus Mozart
Steckbrief

1756	geboren am 27. Januar in Salzburg
	als Dreijähriger erhält er Musikunterricht bei seinem Vater Leopold
1762 – 1766	erste Konzertreisen mit seinem Vater und seiner Schwester
	Maria-Anna (Nannerl) durch Europa, u.a. nach Paris und London
1769	in Salzburg wird der 13-jährige zum Konzertmeister ernannt
	Konzertreise nach Italien
1778	Tod der Mutter in Paris, Hoforganist in Salzburg
1781	Mozart verlässt Salzburg und lebt als freier Künstler in Wien
1782	Heirat mit Konstanze Weber, die ihn viele Jahre überlebt
1787	Mozart wird zum Kaiserlichen Kammermusiker ernannt und
	unterrichtet kurz den 17-jährigen Ludwig van Beethoven
1791	die Komposition seines Requiems bleibt unvollendet
	er stirbt am 5. Dezember und wird in einem Armengrab beerdigt
	der Ort ist nicht bekannt

Vorwort

Wolfgang Amadeus Mozart, wie Haydn und Beethoven, ein Komponist der Klassik, ist einer der bekanntesten und am meisten aufgeführten Musiker überhaupt. Der Reichtum seiner Melodien ist unerschöpflich. Das Besondere an ihm ist, dass er schon in ganz frühen Jahren als Wunderkind das Klavier- und Violinspiel beherrschte. Als Fünfjähriger begann er zu komponieren. Er hatte ein besonders gutes Gehör und Gedächtnis. Sein Vater Leopold stellte ihn schon ab dem sechsten Lebensjahr als hochbegabtes Kind in ganz Europa vor, zum Beispiel 1762 am Hof der Kaiserin Maria-Theresia in Wien.

In seinen Konzerten improvisierte Mozart meist und schrieb diese Stücke später aus dem Gedächtnis auf. Er wurde nur 35 Jahre alt, komponierte aber in seinem Leben über 600 Stücke. Sein Werk umfasst u.a. zahlreiche Symphonien, Klavier- Violin- und Bläserkonzerte, Messen, viele Opern, darunter *Die Zauberflöte*, *Figaros Hochzeit* und *Don Giovanni*, Streichquartette, Kammermusikwerke, Klavierwerke und das berühmte Requiem.
Seine Werke sind im sogenannten Köchelverzeichnis mit der Abkürzung KV gesammelt.

Die meisten Stücke des vorliegenden Heftes stammen aus dem *Londoner Skizzenbuch* mit Kompositionen des Achtjährigen sowie einigen seiner frühen Stücke, die Vater Leopold in das *Notenbuch für Nannerl*, seine Schwester, aufgenommen hat. Leopold hat den jungen Wolfgang unterrichtet und für ihn das *Notenbuch für Wolfgang* angelegt. Fünf Kompositionen daraus, mit denen der Siebenjährige groß geworden ist, sind im Anhang aufgenommen.

Das Heft wird ergänzt durch beliebte Stücke wie Thema und 5. Variation *Ah, vous dirai-je, Maman*, Thema aus dem Variationensatz der A-Dur Sonate KV 331 und den langsamen Satz aus der bekannten Sonate C-Dur KV 545 (Sonata facile).

Zur Ausführung der Stücke

Die Klavierkompositionen von Mozart können alle ohne Pedal gespielt werden. Bei sparsamem Pedalgebrauch ist darauf zu achten, dass eine Dreiklangmelodie nicht als Harmonie zusammen klingt, dass also aus einer Melodie keine Harmonie wird. Die Metronomangaben sind Vorschläge des Herausgebers, die individuell den Fähigkeiten des Spielers angepasst werden können.

Wilhelm Ohmen

Wolfgang Amadeus Mozart
Biography

1756	Born in Salzburg on 27 January
	Started music lessons with his father Leopold at the age of three
1762–1766	First concert tours with his father and his sister Maria-Anna (Nannerl) across Europe, including visits to Paris and London
1769	Appointed as orchestral leader in Salzburg at the age of thirteen Concert tour in Italy
1778	Mother died in Paris; appointed court organist in Salzburg
1781	Mozart left Salzburg to live in Vienna as a freelance artist
1782	Married Konstanze Weber, who outlived him by many years
1787	Mozart appointed as Imperial Chamber Musician; for a short while he gave lessons to the seventeen year-old Ludwig van Beethoven
1791	Composition of his Requiem left incomplete Mozart died on 5 December and was buried in a common grave in an unknown location

Preface

Wolfgang Amadeus Mozart was a classical composer, like Haydn and Beethoven. He remains one of the most celebrated and most often performed composers of all time, inexhaustible in melodic inspiration. Already remarkable as a child prodigy, he mastered the piano and violin at a very early age and began to compose at the age of five, with particularly acute hearing and an excellent memory. From the age of six he toured all over Europe with his father Leopold, for instance demonstrating his gifts at the court of the Empress Maria-Theresia in Vienna in 1762.

Mozart would usually improvise in his concerts and write these pieces down later from memory. He only reached the age of thirty-five, yet composed over six hundred pieces in his lifetime. His works include numerous symphonies, concertos for piano, violin and wind instruments, church masses, many operas - including *The Magic Flute*, *The Marriage of Figaro* and *Don Giovanni*, string quartets, chamber music, piano pieces and the famous Requiem. His works are listed in the Köchel index using the abbreviation K.

Most of the pieces in this book are taken from the *London Sketchbook*, featuring compositions by the eight-year old Mozart and a few of his early pieces, which his father Leopold wrote down in a book of music for Wolfgang's sister Nannerl. Leopold Mozart taught the young Wolfgang and put together a book of music for him, too. Five pieces from that book, a record of the seven-year old's childhood, are included in the Appendix.

The book also contains popular pieces such as the theme and five variations on *Ah, vous dirai-je, Maman* [the tune we know as 'Twinkle, twinkle, little star'], the theme from the variation movement of the Sonata in A major K 331 and the slow movement from the famous Sonata in C major K 545 (*Sonata facile*).

Performing these pieces

All Mozart's piano compositions can be played without the pedal. With sparing use of the pedal, make sure that chordal melodies do not sound together like a harmonization, as melodic lines should not be confused with harmonies. Metronome markings are editorial suggestions that may be adapted to suit the abilities of each player.

Wilhelm Ohmen
Translation: Julia Rushworth

Inhalt / Contents

Anhang / Supplement:

Aus dem Notenbuch für Wolfgang von Leopold Mozart /
From the Music Book for Wolfgang by Leopold Mozart

Menuett / Minuet

KV 1e + f (Trio)

Wolfgang Amadeus Mozart
1756–1791

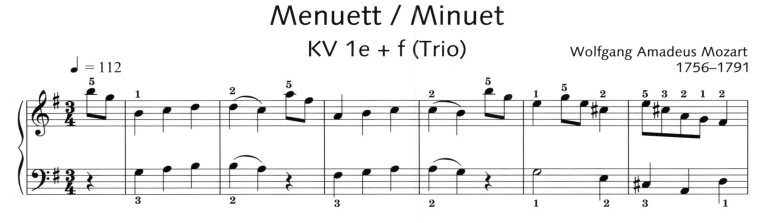

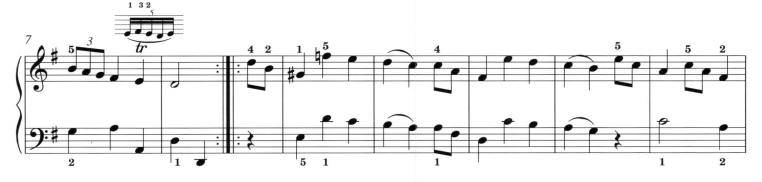

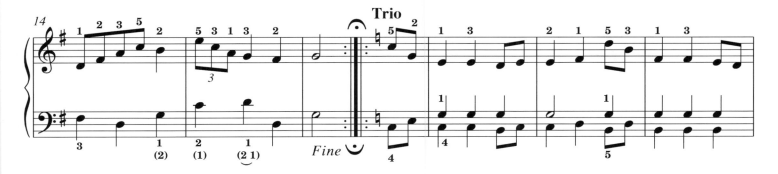

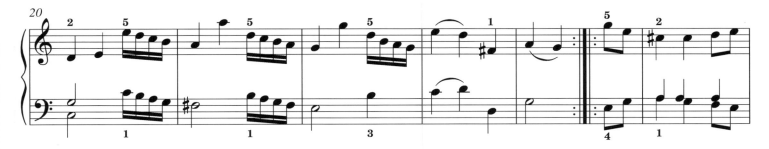

aus / from: W. A. Mozart; Notenbuch für Nannerl / Nannerl's Music Book

Menuett da Capo al Fine

© 2015 Schott Music GmbH & Co. KG, Mainz

Das widerrechtliche Kopieren von Noten ist gesetzlich verboten und kann privat- und strafrechtlich verfolgt werden.
Unauthorised copying of music is forbidden by law, and may result in criminal or civil action.

Menuett / Minuet

KV 2

Wolfgang Amadeus Mozart

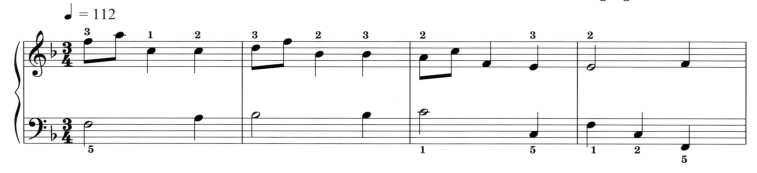

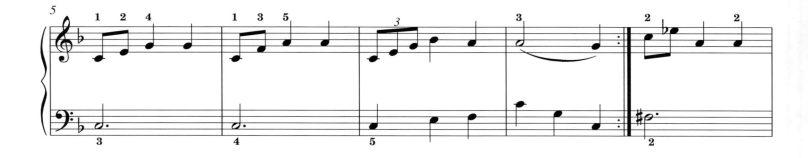

aus / from: W. A. Mozart; Notenbuch für Nannerl / Nannerl's Music Book

© 2015 Schott Music GmbH & Co. KG, Mainz

Allegro
KV 3

Wolfgang Amadeus Mozart

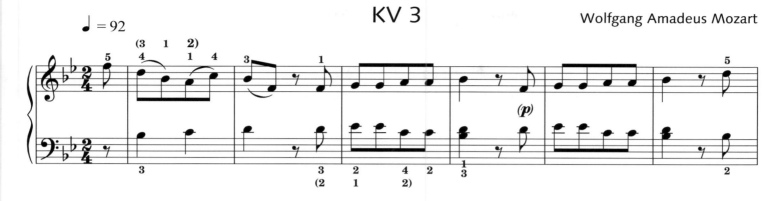

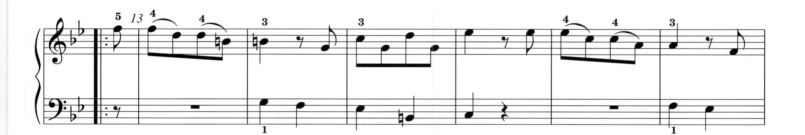

aus / from: W. A. Mozart; Notenbuch für Nannerl / Nannerl's Music Book

© 2015 Schott Music GmbH & Co. KG, Mainz

Menuett / Minuet
KV 5

Wolfgang Amadeus Mozart

aus / from: W. A. Mozart; Notenbuch für Nannerl / Nannerl's Music Book

© 2015 Schott Music GmbH & Co. KG, Mainz

Menuett / Minuet
KV 6

Wolfgang Amadeus Mozart

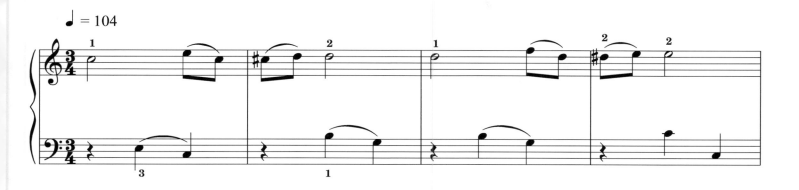

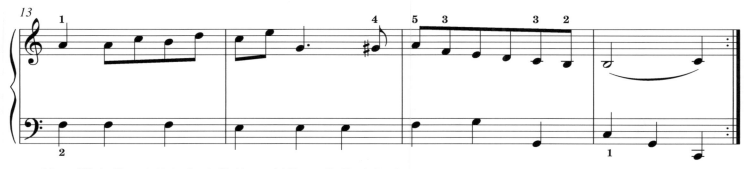

aus / from: W. A. Mozart; Notenbuch für Nannerl / Nannerl's Music Book

© 2015 Schott Music GmbH & Co. KG, Mainz

Menuett / Minuet

KV 7

Wolfgang Amadeus Mozart

aus / from: W. A. Mozart; Notenbuch für Nannerl / Nannerl's Music Book

© 2015 Schott Music GmbH & Co. KG, Mainz

Allegretto
KV 15a

Wolfgang Amadeus Mozart

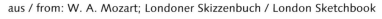

aus / from: W. A. Mozart; Londoner Skizzenbuch / London Sketchbook

* Vorschlag / Grace note

© 2015 Schott Music GmbH & Co. KG, Mainz

Menuett / Minuet
KV 15c

Wolfgang Amadeus Mozart

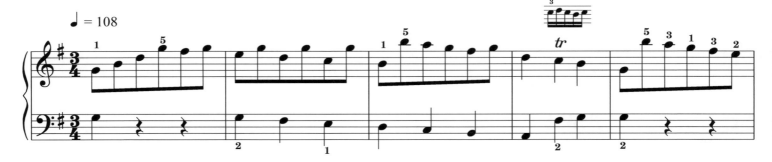

aus / from: W. A. Mozart; Londoner Skizzenbuch / London Sketchbook

© 2015 Schott Music GmbH & Co. KG, Mainz

Rondeau
KV 15d

Wolfgang Amadeus Mozart

aus / from: W. A. Mozart; Londoner Skizzenbuch / London Sketchbook

© 2015 Schott Music GmbH & Co. KG, Mainz

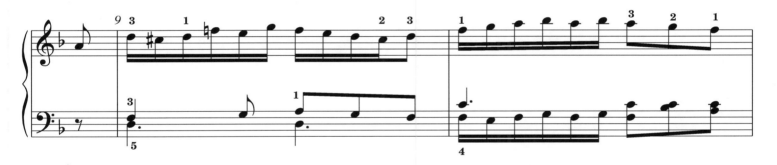

Fine

D. C. al Fine

Kontretanz / Contredance
KV 15e

Wolfgang Amadeus Mozart

aus / from: W. A. Mozart; Londoner Skizzenbuch / London Sketchbook

© 2015 Schott Music GmbH & Co. KG, Mainz

Kontretanz / Contredance
KV 15i

Wolfgang Amadeus Mozart

aus / from: W. A. Mozart; Londoner Skizzenbuch / Londoner Sketchbook

© 2015 Schott Music GmbH & Co. KG, Mainz

Menuett / Minuet
KV 15ff

Wolfgang Amadeus Mozart

aus / from: W. A. Mozart; Londoner Skizzenbuch / London Sketchbook

© 2015 Schott Music GmbH & Co. KG, Mainz

leichter / easier: leichter / easier:

Andante
KV 15mm

Wolfgang Amadeus Mozart

Fine

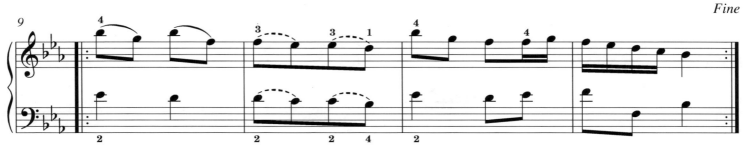

D. C. al Fine

aus / from: W. A. Mozart; Londoner Skizzenbuch / London Sketchbook

© 2015 Schott Music GmbH & Co. KG, Mainz

Menuett / Minuet
KV 15oo

Wolfgang Amadeus Mozart

aus / from: W. A. Mozart; Londoner Skizzenbuch / London Sketchbook

© 2015 Schott Music GmbH & Co. KG, Mainz

Menuett / Minuet

KV 15pp

Wolfgang Amadeus Mozart

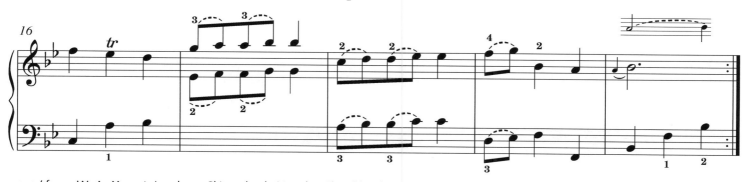

aus / from: W. A. Mozart; Londoner Skizzenbuch / London Sketchbook

© 2015 Schott Music GmbH & Co. KG, Mainz

Menuett / Minuet
KV 15qq

Wolfgang Amadeus Mozart

aus / from: W. A. Mozart; Londoner Skizzenbuch / London Sketchbook

© 2015 Schott Music GmbH & Co. KG, Mainz

Menuett / Minuet
KV 176/3

Wolfgang Amadeus Mozart

aus / from: W. A. Mozart; Elf Menuette / Eleven Minuets

© 2015 Schott Music GmbH & Co. KG, Mainz

Menuett / Minuet
KV 176/7

Wolfgang Amadeus Mozart

aus / from: W. A. Mozart; Elf Menuette / Eleven Minuets

* Vorschlag / Grace Note

© 2015 Schott Music GmbH & Co. KG, Mainz

Menuett / Minuet

Wolfgang Amadeus Mozart

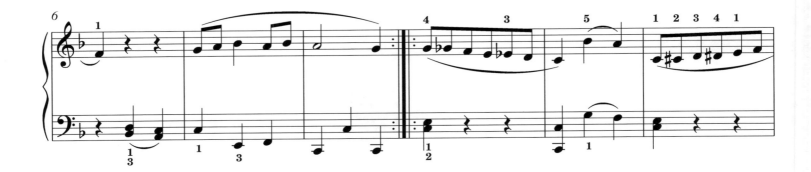

© 2015 Schott Music GmbH & Co. KG, Mainz

Walzer / Waltz

Wolfgang Amadeus Mozart

© 2015 Schott Music GmbH & Co. KG, Mainz

D. C. al Fine

Ah, vous dirai-je, Maman
KV 265 (300e)

Wolfgang Amadeus Mozart

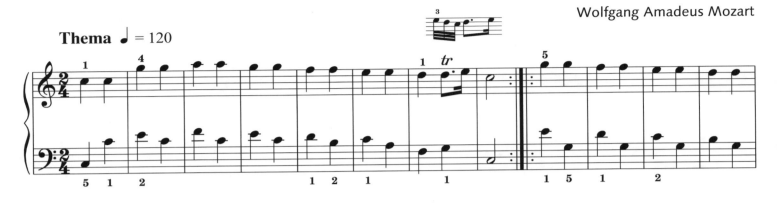

Thema ♩ = 120

Variation V

aus / from: W. A. Mozart; 12 Variationen über das französische Lied / 12 Variations on the French Song

© 2015 Schott Music GmbH & Co. KG, Mainz

Menuett / Minuet
KV 315a (315g)

Wolfgang Amadeus Mozart

♩ = 108

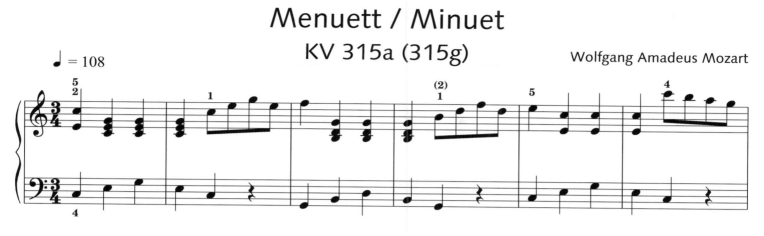

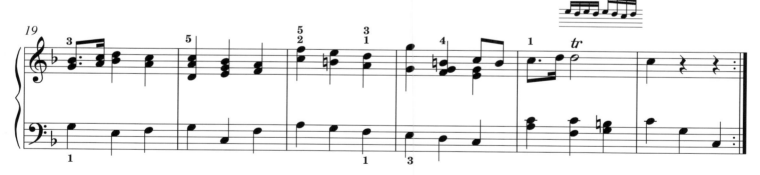

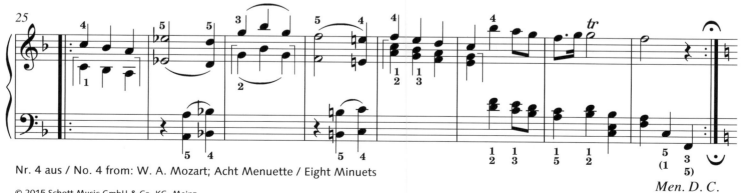

Nr. 4 aus / No. 4 from: W. A. Mozart; Acht Menuette / Eight Minuets

Men. D. C.

© 2015 Schott Music GmbH & Co. KG, Mainz

Andante grazioso
KV 331

Wolfgang Amadeus Mozart

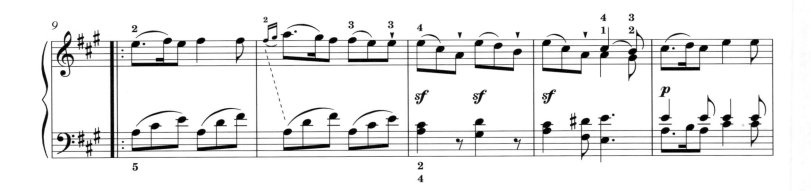

aus / from: W. A. Mozart; Thema des 1. Satzes (Variationen) aus der Sonate A-Dur / Theme of the 1st movement from Sonata A major

© 2015 Schott Music GmbH & Co. KG, Mainz

Polonaise
KV 439b

Wolfgang Amadeus Mozart

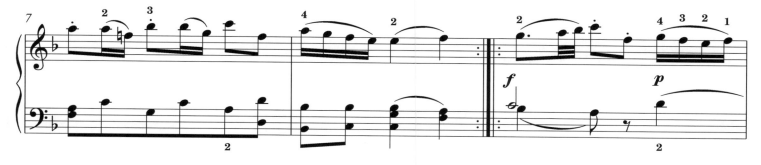

aus / from: W. A. Mozart; Wiener Sonatine Nr. 5 / Vienna Sonatina No. 5

© 2015 Schott Music GmbH & Co. KG, Mainz

Andante
KV 545

Wolfgang Amadeus Mozart

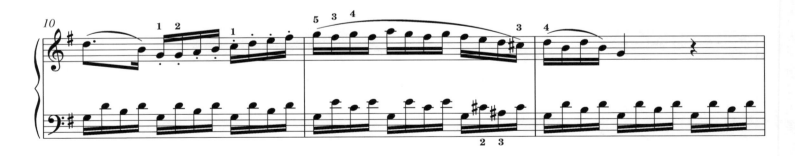

aus / from: W. A. Mozart; Sonate C-Dur KV 545, 2. Satz / Sonata C major, 2nd movement, KV 545

© 2015 Schott Music GmbH & Co. KG, Mainz

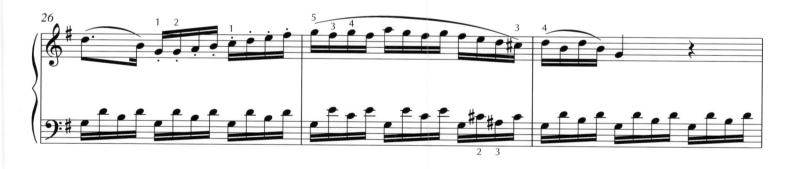

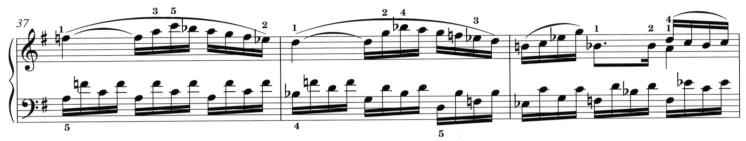

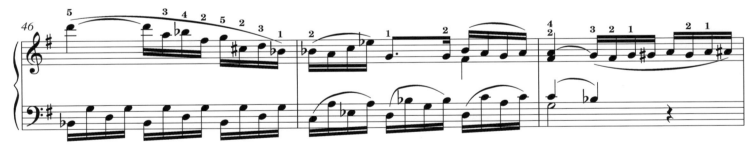

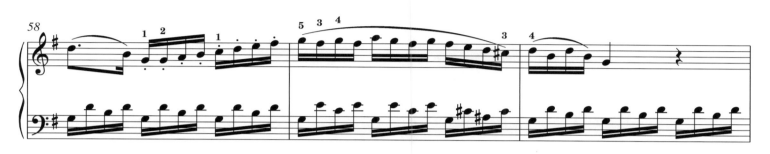

Anhang / Supplement

Fünf Stücke aus dem *Notenbuch für Wolfgang*
Five Pieces from the *Music Book for Wolfgang*

Mozart am Klavier mit Vater Leopold und Schwester Nannerl
Nach einem Aquarell von Louis Carrogis de Camontelle, 1763
Paris. Original im British Museum, London

Bourlesq

Alte Volksweise

© 2015 Schott Music GmbH & Co. KG, Mainz

Menuett / Minuet

Leopold Mozart

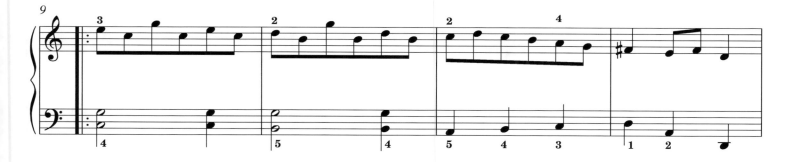

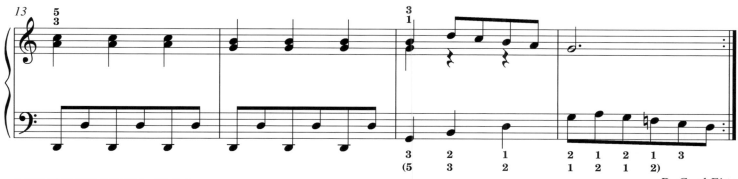

© 2015 Schott Music GmbH & Co. KG, Mainz

D. C. al Fine

Bourrée

Leopold Mozart

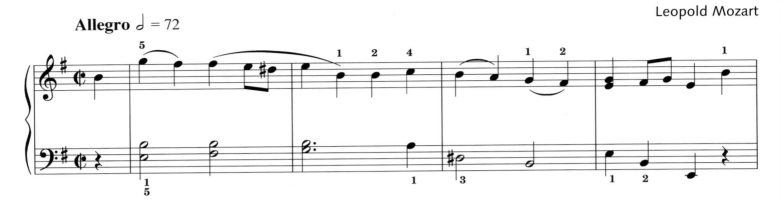

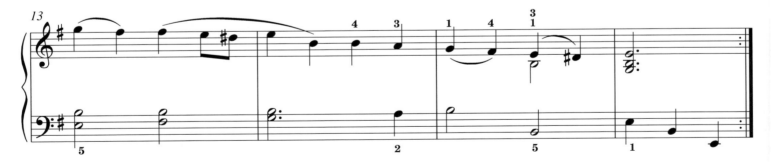

© 2015 Schott Music GmbH & Co. KG, Mainz

Musette

Leopold Mozart

Fine

© 2015 Schott Music GmbH & Co. KG, Mainz

D. C. al Fine

Polonaise

Leopold Mozart

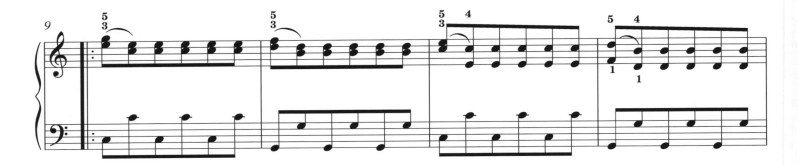

© 2015 Schott Music GmbH & Co. KG, Mainz